1913:
• Rosa Parks born

• Harriet Tubman dies

1914:
• World War I begins in Europe

• George Washington Carver reveals his experiments with peanuts as a crop for southern fields

• Panama Canal opens

1915
• Rocky Mountain National Park established

• Raggedy Ann doll created

1916:
• Beverly Cleary (author of *Ramona* books) born

• National Park Service is created by an Act of Congress

1917:
• United States enters World War I

• Stamps go up to 3 cents

1918: • Daylight saving time begins, instituted as a wartime measure to conserve energy

• Armistice ends hostilities in World War

1919:
• Dial telephones are introduced

• Theodore Roosevelt dies

1920:
• 19th amendment gives women the vote in America

• First commercial radio broadcast

1921:
• Amelia Earhart takes her first flying lesson

• Baby Ruth candy bar introduced

Published by Kansas City Star Books

1729 Grand Boulevard

Kansas City, MO 64108

Copyright © 2010 Kansas City Star Books

First Edition

Edited: Monroe Dodd/PortLight

Design: Jean Donaldson Dodd/PortLight

ISBN 978-1-935362-73-9

Library of Conress Control Number: 2010935079

Printed in the United States of America
by Walsworth Publishing Co. Inc.
Marceline, Mo.

Introductory illustrations

Front cover: Kansas Flint Hills and teenage Mary White
(inset)
Back cover: Mary White at various ages (clockwise from
upper left to middle right), Red Rocks and postcard with
horseshow of rose (center), panorama of downtown Emporia,
early 1900s (bottom).
P. 2-3: Downtown Emporia, 1910s.
P. 4: Mary White, about 2 years old, with her mother, Sallie,
and brother, Bill.
p. 5: Peter Pan statue in Peter Pan Park, Emporia, Kansas.
Sculptor was John Forsythe, Reading, Kansas.

Illustration sources

Emporia State University Archives, Emporia State University:
    William Allen White Collection, courtesy of Christopher Walker:
    Front cover (inset), back cover (top center, top right, middle
    right) 1, 4, 6, 7 (upper), 8 (right and lower left), 9, 12 (top), 13,
    14-15, 16, 17 (lower), 18, 19, 20, 21, 22, 24, 25, 26 (upper), 27,
    29, 30, 31, 32, 33, 34, 35, 36, 37, 39 (typescript), 40, 42 (upper),
    44.
    The Walter M. Anderson Collection: 26 (lower).

Emporia *Gazette*: 10 (lower), 28, 39 (lower right), 41, 46-47.

Lyon County Historical Archives and Museum: Back cover (bottom),
8 (upper left), 38.

Kansas State Historical Society, 2-3, 8 (middle left).

University of Kansas Spencer Research Library, courtesy of
Christopher Walker:
    Cecil E. Carl Collection: 12, 23, back cover (left).
    William Allen White Collection: 10, 43, 45 (bottom).

Kansas Geological Survey: Front cover (background).

John Atherton: 17 (postcard, front and back).

William Allen White House State Historic Site: 33 (inset).

Postcard collection of Loyette Polhans Olson: Back cover (center), 2,
3 (inset), 7 (lower), 12 (middle), 45.

A Prairie Peter Pan

THE STORY OF MARY WHITE

Beverley Olson Buller

★ KANSAS CITY STAR BOOKS

KANSAS CITY, MISSOURI

She was a Peter Pan, who refused to grow up.

You know Peter Pan, don't you? Peter loved adventure almost as much as he loved mischief. He made lots of friends, had lots of fun — and he could fly.

In 1904, Peter Pan first appeared in a play in England. The same year, another Peter Pan was born in a small town on the Kansas prairie. In her short life, this Peter Pan craved adventure and made mischief as eagerly as she made friends. She even found her own way to fly.

The imaginary Peter Pan never grew up. Neither did the Peter Pan of our story. Our Peter Pan lives on because of her father. He was a storyteller, and with his magic he kept her alive and shared her story with us. In her father's own words ...

... She was the happ

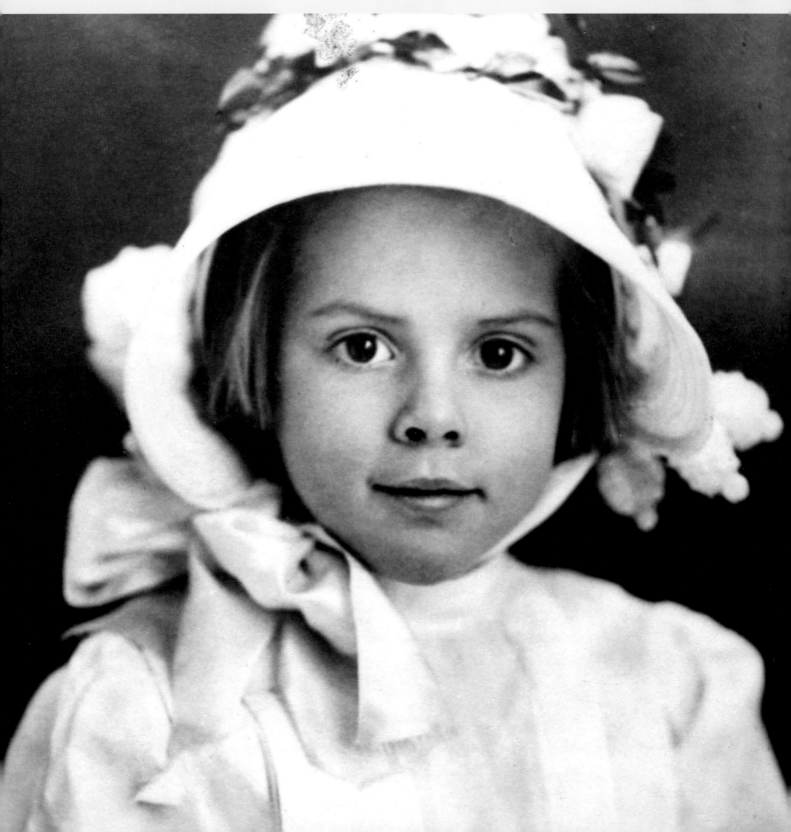

t thing in the world.

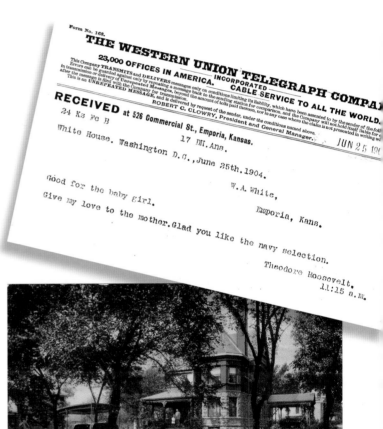

Our Peter Pan was named Mary Katherine White. She was born June 18, 1904. A week later a telegram arrived.

"Good for the baby girl," it read. It was from the president of the United States, Theodore Roosevelt.

Mary's father, William Allen White, owned the newspaper in Emporia, a small Kansas town. The newspaper was called the *Gazette*. It, too, was small, but William Allen White's reputation was big. He was a skilled and famous writer who chose to stay in Kansas instead of moving to a big city. National magazines published his work, and he was the author of three books. He knew people all over the country, and the president was one of them.

Congratulations from the White House for the new baby at Red Rocks.

Home for baby Mary was a big house made with red rock. People called it just that, Red Rocks. There she lived with her father, her mother, Sallie, and her brother, Bill. Bill was 4 when Mary was born.

Mary's father was a famous writer of the early 20th century, William Allen White, top left. When Mary was an infant, center left, she sat for a photograph with her brother and her grandmother, whose name also was Mary White. Grandmother White's house, left, was next door to Red Rocks. Above: Mary with her other grandmother, Frances Lindsay.

Baby Mary was small and weak. People who saw Mary in her baby buggy that first summer might have thought she would not live. She needed good wishes — from the president, from family friends, from everyone.

Mary's mother was weak, too. To help her mother rest and get well, Grandma White took Bill to Colorado. That way, Red Rocks could be a quieter place. It worked. In August, Mary's father wrote Grandma White, "Mary and Sallie are getting strong."

From early in her childhood, Mary loved to ride.

Later that summer, Mary and her mother traveled to Colorado, too. The cool, dry mountain air helped both of them. The family began spending every summer in the mountains to escape the Kansas heat. In years to come, trips to Colorado would bring Mary some of her favorite times.

As she grew, she also had good times in her own neighborhood. Her father recalled ...

... she brought home riotous stories of her adventures.

When Bill went to the river to swim, Mary went, too. When Bill and his friends created plays to perform for parents, Mary took part. She loved roughhousing with her brother, with other children and with the family dog, Teddy. Mary was smaller than other children her age, but her voice was big. She liked to be in the middle of

CELTIC AT LIVERPOOL LANDING STAGE.

Mary and her family traveled across the Atlantic aboard the ocean liner S. S. Celtic. There were plenty of activities for the passengers during the seven-day voyage.

On board S·S· "CELTIC

. . PROGRAMME . .

OF

. . ATHLETIC SPORTS . .

HELD ON BOARD

ON FRIDAY, AUGUST 20th, 1909

COMMENCING AT 3·00 P.M.

COMMITTEE:

HIS GRACE THE DUKE OF NEWCASTLE

MISS O'BRIEN   MR HENRY PHIPPS

MR E T H TALMAGE   DR E S CUNNINGHAM

ABSTRACT OF LOG.

S.S. CELTIC.   COMMANDER—A. E. S. HAMBELTON, R.N.R.

LIVERPOOL TO NEW YORK, AUGUST 14TH, 1909.
PASSED DAUNT'S ROCK LIGHT VESSEL, 9-35 A.M., AUGUST 15TH.

DATE	MILES	LAT.	LONG.	REMARKS.
Aug. 16	446	50.17	19.48	*Moderate W'ly winds and fine*
„ 17	368	48.40	28.50	*Fresh N.W'ly gale and rough sea*
„ 18	406	45.51	38.00	*Moderate to light W'ly winds*
„ 19	390	42.47	46.00	*Moderate W'ly winds and heavy rain*
„ 20	400	41.36	54.30	*Moderate S'ly winds and misty*
„ 21	394	41.13	63.14	*Calm and clear weather*
„ 22	408	40.30	72.09	*Light breeze and clear*

78 *To Ambrose Channel L. V. Arrived at 4-13 p.m. Aug. 22nd.*

DISTANCE—2,890 MILES.   PASSAGE—7 DAYS, 11 HOURS 38 MINUTES.

everything.

There were so many places to explore. Red Rocks had a barn. Grandma built her house next door to Mary's. Mary ran in and out of the barn, and Grandma White's house, and neighbors' houses, too. Weather never dampened Mary's fun. On the third floor of her home was a playroom open to all on rainy days.

Mary went to birthday parties and took piano lessons. Sometimes, piano practice brought tears. It meant that she might miss some outdoor fun.

The White family traveled far beyond their neighborhood, and far beyond their home town. Mary celebrated her fifth birthday in Europe. The Whites sailed from New York on a big ship. On board, Mary took part in all the children's games. With her parents, her brother and Grandma White, she visited Italy, Switzerland, France, England, Wales and Ireland.

Mary's seventh birthday came in the mountains of Colorado. Her father rented a cabin for the whole summer on a hillside near the village of Estes Park. Mary could explore the outdoors to her heart's content. There were horses and burros to ride. Bill hiked and fished. Their father set up a tent to work on the novel he was

Mary with her father and brother. Below: Item from Emporia Gazette.

Americus Thursday afternoon.

Little Mary White, of 927 Ex-change, was bitten by a dog yester-day. They choked the dog to get him away from her, and then she got mad and they had to choke Mary to get her away from the dog and she chased him under a porch and tried to pull him out by the tail to fight him some more. Cer-tainly that child does take after her mother.

Passenger service between

Summers were spent in the cool, high altitudes near Estes Park, Colorado.

writing. Their mother rested.

In the evenings, the children gathered by the fireplace and listened to their mother or father read aloud. The next summer, the family bought the cabin. It became Mary's summer home for the rest of her life.

The Town of Estes Park, Colo., Estes Park, Colo.

Road and Trail Map

OF

ESTES PARK
COLORADO

—AND—

Rocky Mountain National Park

Showing Principal Streams, Lakes,
Mountains, Hotels, Ranches and
Elevations

———

Price 15 Cents

Mary's own copy of a map of the White family's vacation area.

~Winter Fern Lake ~

BIERSTADT LAKE

-Tyndall Glacier-

From FLAT TOP MT.
ALT. 12,300

BEAR LAKE ALT. 9606

Summer

LOCH VALE ALT. 10250

CHASM LAKE ALT. 11950

LONGS PEAK ALT. 14255

ROCKY MOUNTAIN NATIONAL PARK

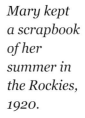

Mary kept a scrapbook of her summer in the Rockies, 1920.

In 1912, Theodore Roosevelt, top right, and his cousin visited the White family at Red Rocks. Mary dressed in stripes and Bill held the family dog, Teddy.

A Prairie Peter Pan

After Mary turned 8, big news came to her town. Theodore Roosevelt was running for president again, and his train came through Emporia. He stopped to visit the Whites. They showed him around town in their buggy after church and served him a big Sunday dinner. Bill ate with the grownups, but Mary chose to eat in the kitchen so she could have all the fried chicken she wanted.

William Allen White worked hard for Theodore Roosevelt, but this time Roosevelt lost the election. After the campaign, Mary's parents needed rest. They rented a vacation cottage in La Jolla, California, and took Mary and Bill with them. Every day the two children played on the beach. Mary finished third grade in La Jolla but kept in touch with her teacher and classmates back home. "I am having a fine time," she wrote them. "I am sending you some shells and hope they have not been crushed." She went on to say, "On our way to school we see many large palms. I wish you could see them."

Sometimes, when her father traveled by train on business, Mary went along. On one

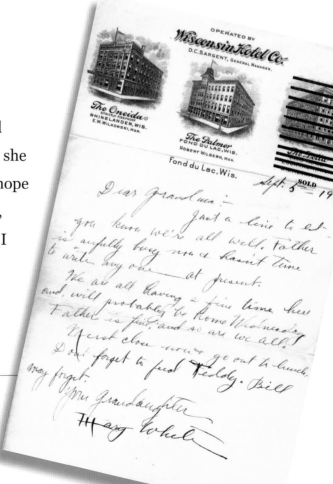

A La Jolla postcard for one of Mary's teachers, above. A letter to Grandma White from Wisconsin, below.

trip, in 1919, she wrote Grandma White from a hotel in Wisconsin: "Don't forget to feed Teddy. Bill may forget." The next year, Mary accompanied her father to New York to preview a movie based on one of his novels.

By the time she reached high school, Mary White had traveled more than most people her age would in their entire lifetime. She could visit even more places in her mind. As her father told it ...

... with all her eagerness for the out-of-doors, she loved books.

Because Mary's father was a writer and her mother was once a schoolteacher, books filled their home. Talk about books filled the air. Mary read her favorite books over and over. Charles Dickens became her favorite author. By the time she was 10, Mary had read books by Mark Twain and Rudyard Kipling. Grandma White read to her *The Wonderful Wizard of Oz* by L. Frank Baum. Other children her age knew those books, but Mary's father knew many of the men who wrote them. Famous authors visited the family in Emporia and in Estes Park.

Mary's adventures in the world and in books made her above average. She joined the Latin Club at the local college while she was still in high school. And Mary had other interests. Her father noticed ...

K-B-D-A

School Series

KANSAS BOOK DEALERS ASSOCIATION

Junior Note
BOOK
No. 70

PROPERTY OF _Mary White_

ADDRESS _____

Emporia Public Schools

SEAL AND MOTTO OF KANSAS

PUPIL'S MONTHLY REPORT

Mary White

...must be returned promptly
...so at the opening of a new

A General Estimate

A cross is placed opposite those traits to which especial attention is called

ATTITUDE TOWARD SCHOOL WORK	First Six Weeks	Second Six Weeks	Third Six Weeks
Wastes Time		X	
Work is Carelessly Done			
Copies; Gets Too Much Help			
Gives Up Too Easily			
Shows Improvement			
Very Commendable	X		
RECITATIONS			
Comes Poorly Prepared			
Appears Not to Try			
Inattentive			
Promotion in Danger			
Capable of Doing Much Better			
Work Shows a Falling Off		X	
Work of Grade Too Difficult			
Showing Improvement			
Very Satisfactory	X		
CONDUCT			
Restless; Inattentive			
Inclined to Mischief			
Rude; Discourteous at Times			
Annoys Others			
Whispers Too Much	X		
Shows Improvement		X	
Very Good			

Emporia City Schools

Mary White

Century School

Grade and Class _5 B_

First Term   Year 1914-1915

SUBJECT	Oct. 16	Nov. 17	Jan. 29	TERM
Reading	I	II+	I	I
Spelling	I+	I	I+	I
Writing	II	III+	II+	II
Arithmetic	II+	I	I	I
Grammar and Comp.	I	I	I	I
Geography	II	II+	II+	II+
Drawing	II	III	II+	II
Music	III+	III+	III	III+
Calisthenics—Rhet'als	I	I	I	I
Nature Study—Phys'y	I+		I	I+
History	I+	I+	I+	
Manual Training				
Home Credit Points*				
Scholarship Average	II+	II	II+	II+
Times Tardy		1		
Days Absent	1½	5		
Deportment	II	I		

*See page two for explanation.

Pansy Petzell Teacher

L. A. LOWTHER, Superintendent

... *she had ... an ambition to draw.*

Mary enjoyed comic books and took a drawing class through the mail. Her schoolbooks showed her love of doodling and her sense of humor. Although her teachers may not have appreciated her work, Mary's art drew interest. At 16, she became assistant editor of the high school yearbook. Her funny sketches appeared in the book that year. Her spirits flew when the sponsor of the local college yearbook asked her to draw for it, too.

Her favorite hobby took her beyond books and art. In her mind, it let her fly. Her father wrote ...

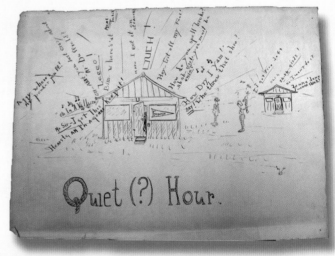

Mary drew friends such as Eleanor Brown, top, and also made comments on life around her in Emporia and Colorado.

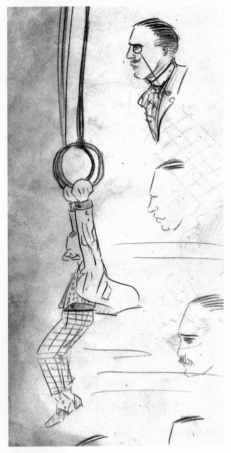

People and places around Emporia, as viewed by Mary White.

... she could ride anything that had four legs and hair.

Some of Mary's earliest adventures occurred in a saddle. Before her feet could reach the stirrups, Mary was led around the block in Emporia on a burro. As she grew, Mary learned to ride the burro herself, and to care for it.

The family kept three burros in Colorado. By the time she was 12, Mary was renting burro rides to tourists. "Mary's heart was wedded to the burros," her father said. Cricket became her favorite.

Back in Emporia, Mary's heart belonged to a Shetland pony, Trixie. The pony and Mary were fast friends. Grandma White even allowed Mary to ride Trixie up the front steps of her house into the living room. Mary gave neighborhood children rides on Trixie.

By the time Mary entered junior high, she rode full-sized horses. One of them, Satin, proved to be too fast. Mary traded him for Hardtack. People in Emporia grew used to seeing Mary on the back of a horse. She still loved giving other children rides.

When no one else was with her, Mary rode fast and recklessly. Riding made Mary feel free. It felt like flying.

It also led to accidents. In April 1920, when Mary was 15, her father wrote to her brother, who was at college: "Mary's horse ran into an automobile the other day and cut her hind leg ... otherwise Mary is all right. This is the regular monthly toot Mary has."

Her father believed that riding made Mary stronger. Her

For Mary White the beginning rider, there were burros. Later, she graduated to horses and included them in her own seal, below.

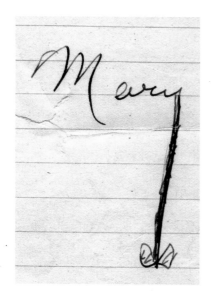

mother worried that she rode too fast. Mary knew only that a horse's legs let her fly.

Mary had her own style, her father recalled ...

... For a decade, the little figure with the long pig-tail and the red hair ribbon has been familiar on the streets of Emporia.

Mary's mother believed children should wear comfortable clothes for play. Mary played much of the time in overalls. As she grew older, Mary still dressed for outdoor adventures. Girls wore skirts in Mary's time. She wore hers in dark colors with a sailor blouse. After school each day, she traded the skirt and blouse for a riding outfit. She ignored styles as they came and went. When short "bobbed" hair became popular for girls, Mary kept hers in a long braid tied with a red ribbon. A cowboy hat topped things off for her rides.

If growing up meant wearing dresses and fancy hairdos, then growing up was not for Mary.

Mary cared more about people than about fashion. In her father's words ...

... She came to know all sorts and conditions of men.

Mary loved to share. She shared her horses and her belongings, too. She led

Unlike her high school classmates, Mary kept her hair long and braided, facing page. Sometimes her braid helped form her signature, above.

singalongs with her ukulele. When a friend wanted to learn to play, Mary taught her and lent her the ukulele. Mary treated other children to ice cream at the store downtown where her father had an account. She wanted everyone to have as much fun as she was having.

Because so many famous people visited her family, Mary felt comfortable with people of all ages. Her high school principal was her friend, even though her pranks sometimes sent her to his office. She became friends with the college music teacher and the pastor of her church. A policeman, Charley O'Brien, watched traffic from a corner not far from her father's newspaper office. As she passed him walking to school or going on a horseback ride, Mary shared stories of her adventures with him.

Mary strumming away, above. One of her pals was policeman Charley O'Brien, left.

Mary wanted no special treatment because her father was famous. She once told a teacher, "I'm sick and tired of being William Allen White's daughter." She wanted people to like her for who she was.

She thought about people who were less fortunate, too. Her father remembered ...

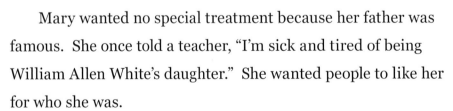

... *The poor she had always with her, and was glad of it.*

When Mary was growing up, public places often had separate areas for white people and black people. Often, black people did not receive equal treatment. Mary's home, Red Rocks, stood near the edge of Emporia's black community. The homes of poor people were nearby. Black children attended her school. She included all children, black and white, in her invitations for horseback rides and ice cream.

Mary learned from watching her parents help their less fortunate neighbors. One neighbor, who was poor, remembered Mary knocking on her porch on hot afternoons to ask for a drink of water. To repay them, on morning rides Mary left vegetables on the porch of the family's home.

Mary became impatient when she found people who needed help but were not getting any. As a teen, she volunteered for the Red Cross. She organized a Christmas meal for poor older people who lived in housing owned by the county.

At Mary's high school, there was a room for girls to study or relax between classes, but only white girls used it. There were five black girls in her class. She asked her principal why black girls didn't have their own room, and started a petition to create one. The dedication in her 1921 high school yearbook said that Mary committed herself "... to the defense of the person or the cause that needed and deserved a friend."

As Mary grew, so did her town. The dirt streets and roads where she galloped her horse were being paved. Automobiles, more of them all the time, honked when horses and wagons blocked their way.

The White family got its first car when Mary was nearly 12. After Bill went to college, Mary took the wheel. Driving was a new way for Mary to fly. And she wasn't alone. As her father said ...

... *Everybody rode with Mary White.*

She shared her car as she shared her horses. Anyone could count on Mary for a ride. When the car was full, kids stood on the running board and hung on. If the car stopped by the ice cream parlor, so much the better. The family auto, her father said, "was her social life."

Mary drove a car as impulsively as she rode her horse. Driver's education didn't exist in Mary's day. She hit curbs often. Sometimes she had only one hand on the wheel. Mary's parents could get her a slower horse, but not a slower car. Soon they insisted that an older friend drive the car if Mary wanted to take it.

By the time the White family got a new car a few years later, an older Mary took the wheel again.

She still laughed at the idea of getting hurt. If you rode with Mary White, accidents could happen!

"Mary never thought of consequences," a friend recalled.

Like Peter Pan, Mary loved a clever prank. Her father summed up her love of fun this way ...

... *She was mischievous without malice, as full of faults as an old shoe.*

In elementary school, Mary got into more than one scuffle.

Her first year in high school, Mary got into a wrestling match with a girl from the

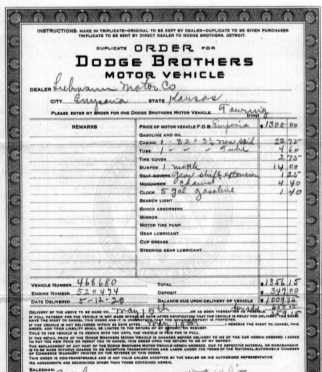

Quite a combination: Mary and cars, above and left. The Whites' contract for a new car, below.

THE
TRUE BLUE

Y. W. C. A. Paper for High School Girls. Issued Thrice a Year by the West Central Field Committee, 321 McClintock Bldg., Denver, Colo. Price 10c a Copy.

THE TRUE B

Mary White Has Learned When to Put on the Brakes!

O, Mary, Mary,
If you are not wary,
Your obituary
    True Blue will yet write.
Indeed, we are merry
You're in no cemetery,
For without you
    We'd be in a plight.

We are happy to tell you that Mary
White of Emporia is safe and sound,
alive and well, except for a bruised
arm and a slightly damaged finger.

As you know, Mary has an adven-
turous spirit. We never asked her how
she acquired her maimed nose at Est
Park, but now we suspect that it mig
have come from trying to dive off Ch
Narrows on Long's Peak to
Lake, 10,000 feet below! Of cou
we don't know, but it seems likely.

Not long ago—in fact, just a
days after she had dashed off the
toons for True Blue—Mary, with three guests, was co
the White car down the slope near the Shady Slope
northeast of Emporia. Suddenly Mary realized that the
was going by too fast, and she threw on the brakes
a small-sized mountain appeared in the road. The ca
skiddish, turned around twice, cramped two of its wheel
over in a spasm of agony and finally lost consciousne
middle of an irrigation ditch. So much for the car.
know yet how much!) The three guests, a trifle b
were thrown clear of the wreckage, but Mary's red h
were untied and one of her arms was caught under
wheel. Otherwise she is the same little girl.

Congratulations, Mary, for sticking to the wh
last girl was out!

"OUR MARY"

"Mu
Th
We
We

A
meet

INSTRUCTIONS: MAKE IN TRIPLICATE—ORIGINAL TO BE KEPT BY DEALER—DUPLICATE TO BE GIVEN PURCHASER
TRIPLICATE TO BE SENT BY DIRECT DEALER TO DODGE BROTHERS, DETROIT.

DUPLICATE ORDER FOR
DODGE BROTHERS
MOTOR VEHICLE

DEALER *Liebmann Motor Co*
CITY *Emporia*   STATE *Kansas*
PLEASE ENTER MY ORDER FOR ONE DODGE BROTHERS MOTOR VEHICLE *Touring*

REMARKS		
	PRICE OF MOTOR VEHICLE F.O.B. *Emporia*	$1305 00
	GASOLINE AND OIL	
	CASING *1 - 32 x 3½ non skid*	22 75
	TUBE *1 - - - - tube*	4 60
	TIRE COVER	2 75
	BUMPER *1 nickel*	14 00
	SEAT COVERS *gray shift extension*	1 25
	MONOGRAM *chassis*	4 40
	CLOCK *5 gal gasoline*	1 40
	SEARCH LIGHT	
	SHOCK ABSORBERS	
	MIRROR	
	MOTOR TIRE PUMP	
	GEAR LUBRICANT	
	CUP GREASE	
	STEERING GEAR LUBRICANT	

VEHICLE NUMBER *466680*	TOTAL	$1356 15
ENGINE NUMBER *520474*	DEPOSIT	347 00
DATE DELIVERED *5-12-20*	BALANCE DUE UPON DELIVERY OF VEHICLE	$1009 15

DELIVERY OF THE ABOVE TO BE MADE ON *May 15th*   OR AS SOON THEREAFTER AS POSSIBLE.
IF FULL PAYMENT FOR THE VEHICLE IS NOT MADE WITHIN 30 DAYS AFTER NOTIFICATION THAT THE VEHICLE IS READY FOR DELIVERY, YOU
HAVE THE RIGHT TO CANCEL THIS ORDER AND IT IS UNDERSTOOD THAT THE ADVANCE DEPOSIT IS FORFEITED.
IF THE VEHICLE IS NOT DELIVERED WITHIN 30 DAYS AFTER .... I RESERVE THE RIGHT TO CANCEL THIS
ORDER, AND YOUR LIABILITY SHALL BE LIMITED TO THE RETURN OF MY DEPOSIT, ON REQUEST.
TITLE TO THE VEHICLE IS TO REMAIN WITH YOU UNTIL THE VEHICLE IS PAID FOR IN FULL.
IF THE RETAIL PRICE OF THE DODGE BROTHERS MOTOR VEHICLE HEREIN ORDERED IS CHANGED BEFORE DELIVERY TO ME OF THE CAR HEREIN ORDERED, I AGREE
TO PAY THE NEW PRICE OR PERMIT YOU TO CANCEL THIS ORDER UPON THE RETURN TO ME OF MY DEPOSIT.
THE REPLACEMENT OF ANY PART OF THE DODGE BROTHERS MOTOR VEHICLE HEREIN ORDERED, DUE TO DEFECTIVE MATERIAL OR WORKMANSHIP,
IS TO BE MADE WITHOUT CHARGE TO ME EXCEPTING TRANSPORTATION AND LABOR UNDER THE TERMS OF THE NATIONAL AUTOMOBILE CHAMBER
OF COMMERCE WARRANTY PRINTED ON THE REVERSE OF THIS ORDER.
THIS ORDER IS NON-TRANSFERABLE AND IS NOT VALID UNLESS ACCEPTED BY THE DEALER OR HIS AUTHORIZED REPRESENTATIVE.
NO AGREEMENTS ARE RECOGNIZED OTHER THAN THOSE CONTAINED HEREIN.

SALESMAN: *E. A. L.*   PURCHASER: *W. A. White*
ACCEPTED *April 14* 19*20*   STREET ADDRESS
DEALER   CITY *Emporia*   STATE *Kans.*
PER:

FORM B 2888 100M 10-18

Mary's humor was a "continual bubble of joy," her father said. One day in Colorado, she played Juliet to a friend's Romeo, facing page.

other side of town. The winner would be top girl in the class. The two were surrounded by a cheering crowd of girls, but the noise brought the gym teacher. She stopped the match and made the two girls shake hands. When the principal, Mr. Brown, showed up, the girls assured him it was all in fun.

A friend found a dead mouse in her apron pocket in sewing class. She knew only one person who would see that kind of thing as a joke.

Another friend remembered a dare that caused her to climb down by rope from Mary's third-floor bedroom.

Mary wasn't afraid of heights. When she was 14, she tagged along with her brother and a pal as they hiked up Longs Peak in Rocky Mountain National Park. The two boys thought Mary would tire and stop along the way. They'd meet her as they made their way back down.

Finally, the boys reached the peak at 14,255 feet. As they prepared to descend, they heard a cry: "Yoo-hoo!" It was Mary, her face glowing. She had made it all the way to the top.

In Estes Park one summer, Mary and a friend hitched a ride in the back of a mail carrier's wagon. Under the seat they found a large box of candy. After the carrier dropped the girls off, he saw the candy was missing. He turned and caught up with them, and the girls admitted taking it. Mary promised to send him a nicer box when she got back to Kansas. She kept her promise. He kept his promise not to tell her father — until long afterward. The story made a sweet 70th birthday present for William Allen White more than two decades later.

One thing Mary did not joke about was her horse. A fellow rider remembered what happened when a boy threw a clod of dirt at Mary's horse. Still on horseback, she chased the boy up on his porch and into his house.

One of her high school teachers said of Mary, "She liked to make people think she was mean, but she really wasn't mean, only a prankster."

Fathers see what they want in their little girls. According to Mary's father ...

... the 'boy proposition' didn't interest her — yet.

At 16, Mary acted much as she always had. But friends noticed small changes.

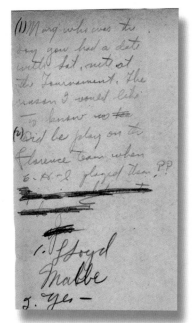

One friend saw Mary with a boy from out of town. To another, Mary showed an interest in face cream. She wrote an essay in language class suggesting girls pay on dates with boys.

Other girls went to dances at the local hangout. Mary surprised many when she showed up at one with her brother, Bill. She wore a long embroidered dress. After one dance, they disappeared. Mary's mother may have provided the dress and ordered the dance. Mary would have to find her own way to remain a Peter Pan once her teenage years were over.

For now, there was her horse. Her father recalled one day in particular, when ...

... She climbed into her khakis ... and hurried to get to her horse and be out on the dirt roads

On May 10, 1921, Mary joined the yearbook staff for a work session in Miss Potter's room. Mr. Brown called for her to come to his office. He had seen a sketch Mary

Telling the name of her date, above. On horseback in the countryside, facing page.
Horseshoe hung by Mary at Red Rocks, inset

In her school days.

had done for the yearbook. It showed a ballerina, only Mr. Brown's photo was pasted where the ballerina's head should have been. Mr. Brown told her it could not go in the yearbook.

Mary returned to the staff session, not understanding her principal's feelings. She had meant it all in fun.

It was time for a horseback ride. At home, she changed out of her skirt and into riding pants. Up on her horse, Hardtack, she headed along Merchant Street for the countryside north of town, waving her cowboy hat and greeting everyone she saw along the way. She wasn't flying – yet – but the horse was loping along.

A boy she knew was riding his bicycle, throwing copies of her father's newspaper onto subscribers' lawns. She turned to wave at him.

When she waved, she used the hand holding the bridle. That confused Hardtack. The horse veered to the side — straight into a low-hanging branch of a catalpa tree. Mary's head hit the branch hard. Stunned, she slid off the horse, staggered, and fell to the ground.

Sickness kept Mary out of early classes on May 9, 1921.

Passers-by loaded Mary in their car. Later, a boy found Hardtack wandering several blocks north and tied her up.

Mary was taken home to her mother. That spring, home for the Whites was the house on the other side of Grandma White's. They had moved because Red Rocks was getting a makeover. Now Mary lay unconscious in the front room of the temporary home. At first, it appeared to be just another of Mary's accidents. Her mother said so in a telegram to her father, who was on a trip to the East Coast.

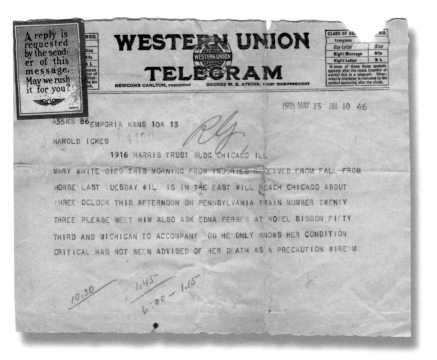

A friend would break the news of Mary's death to her father in Chicago.

"No scars but severe shock," Sallie White wrote. "Horse absolutely has to go."

Mary did not wake up. The family doctor X-rayed her head and found that her skull was fractured. Mary's father and brother received telegrams saying she had taken a turn for the worse. Both headed for Emporia. Both arrived too late.

The family doctor could do nothing for Mary. Early on the morning of May 13, she died.

That afternoon, Mary White's death made news across the country. Her father remembered what happened in the days afterward …

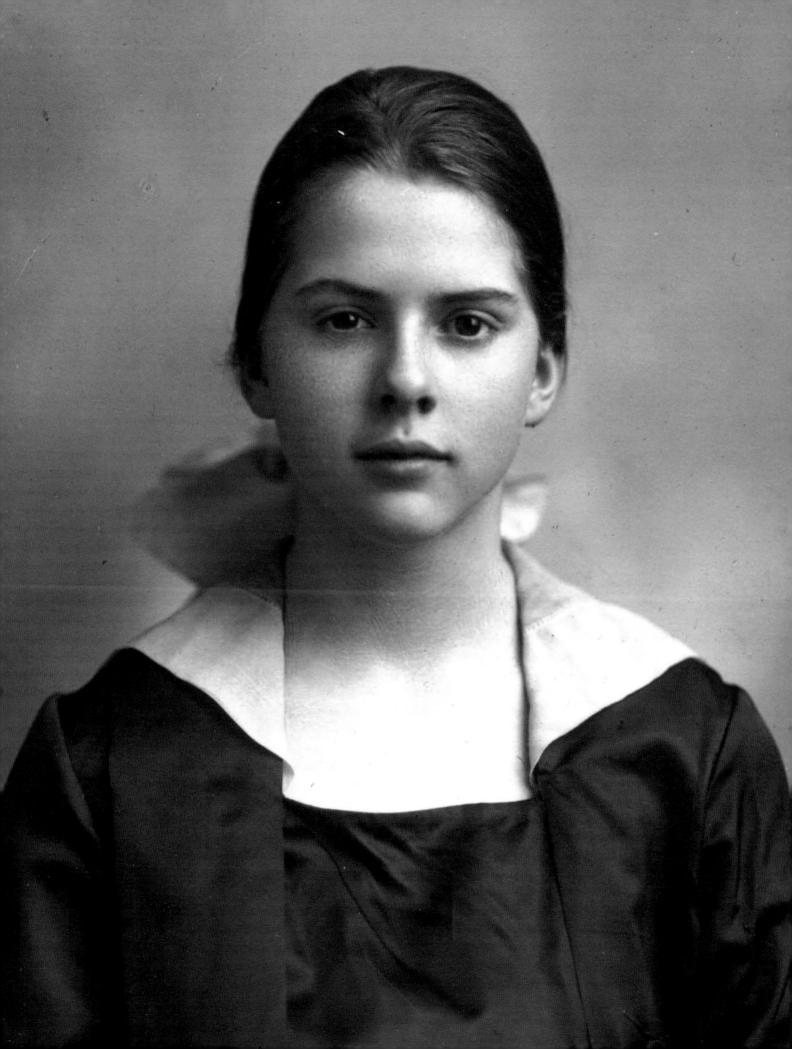

... *Her funeral yesterday at the Congregational Church was as she would have wished it.*

Her family planned a simple service. Friends gathered at her church. Her pastor spoke of love. Flowers were few. Her brother, her principal, and some of her adult friends carried the coffin. High school classmates recited the Lord's Prayer. Mary's favorite classical music, selected with help from the college music teacher, filled the air.

Her friend Charley O'Brien, tears running down his face, directed traffic around the church.

Mary White was buried in Maplewood Cemetery on the north edge of town.

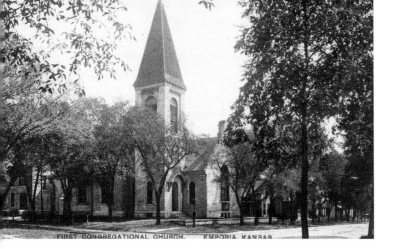

Mary's funeral took place here.

'Mary White'

The day after her funeral, William Allen White and Sallie White went to the office of their newspaper, the *Gazette*. Behind a closed door, with Sallie's help, William Allen White wrote an essay about their daughter. He entitled it simply "Mary White." It appeared in their newspaper May 17, 1921.

People who had known Mary smiled as they read the details of her life. They wept as they read again about her death. Writing the article helped her father get back to work and helped the people of Emporia put Mary to rest.

Yet the touching essay, written from her parents' hearts, did not stay in Emporia. "Mary White" next appeared in *The Kansas City Star*. Then a newspaper in New York City reprinted it. By June 1921, it was showing up in newspapers across the United

MARY WHITE

The Associated Press reports Carrying the news of Mary's White's death declared that it ####### came as the result of a fall from a horse. How she would have hooted at that. She never fell from a horse in her life. Horses have fallen on her and with her-- "I'm always trying to hold 'em in my lap," she used to say. But she was proud of few things,, and one was that she could ride anything that had four legs and hair.. Her death resulted not from a fall, but from a blow on the head which fractured her skull, and the blow came from the limb of an overhanging tree on the parking.

The last hour of her life was typical of its happiness.. She came home from a day's work at school topped off by a hard grind with the copy on the High School Annual,, and felt that a ride would refresh her.. She climbed into her khaki chattering to her mother ############## about the work she was doing, and hurried' to get her horse and be out in the dirt roads for the country air and the joyous green fields, A she rode through the town on an easy gallop she kept She knew every one in town. For a decade the little pig-tail and the red hair ribbon has been familiar ria and #### she got in the way of speaking to those She passed the Kerrs in front of the Normal library, passed Mrs. Dusk a few f#### hundred feet further on, The horse was prancing and as she turned into north Mer her cow boy hat, and the horse swung into a lope. She and waved her cowboy hat at them ####, still moving g Street. A Gazette carrier passed-- a high school boy at him, but with her bridle hand; the horse veered qu the parking where the low hanging limb faced her, and waving the blow came. But she did not fall from the h slipped off, dazed a bit staggered and fell in a f recovered consciousness. But ######## she did not neither was she riding fast. A year or so ago she use that habit was broken, and she used the horse to fresh hard exercise and to work off a certain surp

and grips alone.

MARY WHITE DEAD

Mary Katherine White, only daughter of Mr. and Mrs. W. A. White, died at 5:30 o'clock this morning from an injury received in a fall from a horse Tuesday evening. Her skull was fractured. The exact nature of her injury was not determined until an X-ray picture was taken Wednesday. Yesterday her condition became worse, and Mr. White, who was in the East, and her brother, William, a student at Harvard, were notified. Mr. White will arrive in Emporia tomorrow afternoon and William White is expected tomorrow night or Sunday morning.

The accident which caused her death occurred in a yard on North Merchant Street near the Normal.

The horse she was riding suddenly turned into a driveway, ran into the yard and struck a

With Sallie White's help, Will wrote an enduring remembrance of Mary.

She Died in the Spring

By ENSWORTH REISNER

WHEN THE LEAVES came out on the trees and the grass was green, evenings brought a soft glisten to the eyes of Mary White. She was a junior in high school and it was spring.

All the world was opening up. Her father was the famed William Allen White, editor of *The Emporia Gazette*. His editorials from that small Kansas city had made news around the nation. His counsels were listened to by president and politician. And he loved his daughter, Mary, more than life itself.

Mary was worthy of his love—popular, a good student, athletically inclined. She loved horses and rode them well. One of the familiar sights in Emporia was Mary, mounted on her favorite horse, riding through the streets, headed for a brisk gallop on the outlying country roads.

Vacation was at hand and Mary went on a horseback ride. She hit her head on the limb of a tree and fell, never to wake again. She died in the spring.

The next day the whole town mourned—most of all, her father. But he was a newspaperman. Obituaries are customary in newspapers. Reports of funerals are required. White ran a paper. But who would write this obituary? The day after the funeral William Allen White, himself, did the story—of Mary's death, her burial, and her own philosophy of life.

What the editor and father wrote has become one of the great classics of American newspaper writing. It was a straight newspaper account of what occurred, but also a loving appreciation of the girl who died in the

After young Mary White died, her Kansas editor-father wrote a memorable tribute reprinted on the following pages.

springtime of her life. It described the funeral, the affection of her friends and classmates, the reaction of the townspeople.

But what of the parents? How did her father feel? What enabled him to write with such depth of beauty at a time of grievous personal loss?

There are many persons who die in the springtime of their lives and we, the living, must live on. How do we do it? These are the questions which run through my mind each time I read White's editorial and silently shed a tear for his daughter.

One day I rummaged through some old letters my father had left in a cardboard file holder, rusted with age. I found a letter dated July 14, 1921, and signed: W. A. White. The letterhead was *The Emporia Gazette*. Apparently my father had written a letter of condolence to his old

Her father's loving essay about Mary appeared in magazines, newspapers and books, particularly textbooks. Because the essay appeared in a textbook used by the college she meant to attend, her class dedicated the yearbook to her.

States. Magazines asked to reprint it. Before the year ended, Mary's father approved the use of the editorial in a book of collected essays. Soon it appeared in four reading books used in high school and college. For two decades, her father and mother kept track and found that the article had appeared in more than 40 such books.

The soul of her ...

After the funeral, one of Mary's friends found William Allen White on her front porch. Tears filled his eyes. He had come to ask for Mary's ukulele, which the friend had borrowed. It would help him and Sallie remember her.

Less than a month after Mary died, the school board approved the room for black girls at the high school, the one for which Mary had fought. As the *Gazette* reported, "The room will be dedicated to the memory of Mary White, which would have pleased her more than anything else that could have been done in the high school."

As planned, Mary's cartoons appeared in the 1921 yearbook. The staff dedicated it to her.

Friends from Estes Park sent letters expressing sorrow about her death. One young man wrote that he would care for Cricket, her burro.

> **Wanted—A Picture.**
>
> If you are a High School or a Normal student, perhaps some time or other you have taken a kodak picture of Mary White. Her parents have no picture taken this year, and few of last year. If you have a kodak picture of her—either alone or in a group—no matter how festive and gay it may seem, it would be a great kindness to leave it at the Gazette office or with her parents at 913 Exchange. And if you have the film from which the picture is made, so much better.
>
> **Dramatics.**

"I know of nothing that would make Mary more happy," her father replied. "From the time she was twelve years old until her death, I think she loved Cricket the donkey better than any other ... thing in the world."

That summer and for many summers after, Mary's family did not visit their cabin in Colorado. Instead, her mother and father moved into their remodeled home in Emporia.

Without Mary, though, things were much too quiet. Mary had designed her own

The room at Red Rocks that would have been Mary's, top. Her grave, above.

room for the third floor. It would look like the main room of the family's cabin in the mountains. In the new room, Mary's bed would fit on a frame that would slide into the wall. Now Mary's room held the furnishings and belongings she had left behind. Her mother used it as a place to sew. Large windows facing south brought in cheerful sunlight.

The next year, when Mary's classmates graduated from high school, her parents did something Mary might have done. They held a graduation party at their home and treated everyone to a movie at a downtown theater.

After graduation, Mary had planned to attend college in New England. Even though she never arrived, Wellesley College dedicated its yearbook in 1926 – the year she would have graduated – to Mary White.

In Emporia, Mary's parents donated money for a park in her memory. They asked for it to be named Peter Pan Park.

Through the years, William Allen White's essay was read by generation after generation. It was collected in textbooks and inspired many students. One of them even made a movie based on it.

In his autobiography, William Allen White wrote: "Probably if anything I have written ... survives more than a decade beyond my life's span, it will be the thousand words or so that I hammered out on my typewriter that bright May morning under the shadow and agony of Mary's death."

He was right.

The original Peter Pan had this answer for people who asked where he lived: "Second on the right and then straight on till morning!"

Mary White, our prairie Peter Pan, lives forever at a different place – in the timeless words of her loving father.

Dedication

TO MARY WHITE, our schoolmate, whom we have come to admire, we dedicate this book. She was the embodiment of those things that in the lives of young people are essential. She was the outstanding champion of the Down and Out and of the clean of mind and the pure of heart. To her there was nothing so distasteful as an unwholesome story. Her whole being revolted against unclean thinking. Her emotions and her instincts led her into a finer region of human living. If she seemed not to appreciate the regular channels of moral or spiritual activities it was only a seeming. Down deep in her heart might be found a wholesome and a dominating respect for the fine and decent things in life. She always stood for things that were worth while and gave herself unafraid to the defense of the person or the cause that needed and deserved a friend. It is such personalities who stand in the breach when the right things are in danger and who become the law to the life that has no law in itself. And so to a democrat unafraid, with a great heart and a strong, clean mind, and a dominating will, we dedicate in love and with admiration this our 1921 Re-Echo.

JOHN H. J. RICE.

Emporia, May 18, 1921.

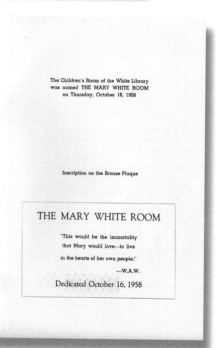

This tribute written by William Allen White to his daughter, Mary, was first published in the *Emporia Gazette*. The original copy is on display in the William Allen White Library.

The Children's Room of the White Library was named THE MARY WHITE ROOM on Thursday, October 16, 1958

Inscription on the Bronze Plaque

THE MARY WHITE ROOM

"This would be the immortality that Mary would love—to live in the hearts of her own people."

—W.A.W.

Dedicated October 16, 1958

Preceding page: Mary's stirrups. Top: Her high school dedicated its 1921 yearbook to her. In 1958 Kansas State Teachers College, now Emporia State University, named a room at its library in her memory.

THE EMPORIA GAZETTE

W. A. WHITE, EDITOR AND OWNER
W. E. HUGHES, MANAGER
EMPORIA, KANSAS

March 29, 1929.

Mr. Oliver Atherton, Mayor,
And
The City Commissioners,
Emporia, Kansas.

Gentlemen:

Mrs. White and Bill and I would like to have the Park just south of Emporia, on the Brown and Randolph tract, known as "The Peter Pan Park". It is given and is being designed for children, and Peter Pan is their guardian spirit.

Sincerely yours,

W A White

WAW/MY.

Peter Pan Park in Emporia, made for children in memory of Mary White.

MARY WHITE

The Associated Press reports carrying the news of Mary White's death declared that it came as the result of a fall from a horse. How she would have hooted at that! She never fell from a horse in her life. Horses have fallen on her and with her—"I'm always trying to hold 'em in my lap," she used to say. But she was proud of few things, and one was that she could ride anything that had four legs and hair. Her death resulted not from a fall, but from a blow on the head which fractured her skull, and the blow came from the limb of an overhanging tree on the parking.

The last hour of her life was typical of its happiness. She came home from a day's work at school, topped off by a hard grind with the copy on the High School Annual, and felt that a ride would refresh her. She climbed into her khakis, chattering to her mother about the work she was doing, and hurried to get her horse and be out on the dirt roads for the country air and the radiant green fields of the spring. As she rode through the town on an easy gallop she kept waving at passers-by. She knew everyone in town. For a decade the little figure with the long pig-tail and the red hair ribbon has been familiar on the streets of Emporia, and she got in the way of speaking to those who nodded at her. She passed the Kerrs, walking the horse, in front of the Normal Library, and waved at them; passed another friend a few hundred feet further on, and waved at her. The horse was walking and, as she turned into North Merchant Street she took off her cowboy hat, and the horse swung into a lope. She passed the Tripletts and waved her cowboy hat at them, still moving gaily north on Merchant Street. A Gazette carrier passed—a High School boy friend—and she waved at him, but with her bridle hand; the horse veered quickly, plunged into the parking where the low-hanging limb faced her, and,

while she still looked back waving, the blow came. But she did not fall from the horse; she slipped off, dazed a bit, staggered and fell in a faint. She never quite recovered consciousness.

But she did not fall from the horse, neither was she riding fast. A year or so ago she used to go like the wind. But that habit was broken, and she used the horse to get into the open to get fresh, hard exercise, and to work off a certain surplus energy that welled up in her and needed a physical outlet That need has been in her heart for years. It was back of the impulse that kept the dauntless, little brown-clad figure on the streets and country roads of this community, and built into a strong, muscular body what had been a frail and sickly frame during the first years of her life. But the riding gave her more than a body. It released a gay and hardy soul. She was the happiest thing in the world. And she was happy because she was enlarging her horizon. She came to know all sorts and conditions of men; Charley O'Brien, the traffic cop, was one of her best friends. W. L. Holtz, the Latin teacher, was another. Tom O'Connor, farmer-politician, and Rev. J. H. J. Rice, preacher and police judge, and Frank Beach, music master, were her special friends, and all the girls, black and white, above the track and below the track, in Pepville and Stringtown, were among her acquaintances. And she brought home riotous stories of her adventures. She loved to rollick; persiflage was her natural expression at home. Her humor was a continual bubble of joy. She seemed to think in hyperbole and metaphor. She was mischievous without malice, as full of faults as an old shoe. No angel was Mary White, but an easy girl to live with, for she never nursed a grouch five minutes in her life.

With all her eagerness for the out-of-doors, she loved books. On

her table when she left her room were a book by Conrad, one by Galsworthy, "Creative Chemistry" by E. E. Slossen, and a Kipling book. She read Mark Twain, Dickens and Kipling before she was 10—all of their writings. Wells and Arnold Bennett particularly amused and diverted her. She was entered as a student in Wellesley in 1922; was assistant editor of the High School Annual this year, and in line for election to the editorship of the Annual next year. She was a member of the executive committee of the High School Y. W. C. A.

Within the last two years she had begun to be moved by an ambition to draw. She began as most children do by scribbling in her school books, funny pictures. She bought cartoon magazines and took a course—rather casually, naturally, for she was, after all, a child with no strong purposes—and this year she tasted the first fruits of success by having her pictures accepted by the High School Annual. But the thrill of delight she got when Mr. Ecord, of the Normal Annual, asked her to do the cartooning for that book this spring, was too beautiful for words. She fell to her work with all her enthusiastic heart. Her drawings were accepted, and her pride—always repressed by a lively sense of the ridiculousness of the figure she was cutting—was a really gorgeous thing to see. No successful artist ever drank a deeper draught of satisfaction than she took from the little fame her work was getting among her schoolfellows. In her glory, she almost forgot her horse—but never her car.

For, she used the car as a jitney bus. It was her social life. She never had a "party" in all her nearly seventeen years—wouldn't have one; but she never drove a block in the car in her life that she didn't begin to fill the car with pick-ups! Everybody rode with Mary White—white and black, old and young, rich and poor, men and women. She liked nothing better than to fill the car full of long-legged High School boys and an occasional girl, and parade the town. She never had a "date," nor went to a dance, except once with her brother, Bill, and the "boy proposition" didn't interest her—yet. But young people — great spring-breaking, varnish-cracking, fender-bending, door-sagging carloads of "kids" gave her great pleasure. Her zests were keen. But the most fun she ever had in her life was acting as chairman of the committee that got up the big turkey dinner for the poor folks at the county home; scores of pies, gallons of slaw; jam, cakes, preserves, oranges and a wilderness of turkey were loaded in the car and taken to the county home. And, being of a practical turn of mind, she risked her own Christmas dinner by staying to see that the poor folks actually got it all. Not that she was a cynic; she just disliked to tempt folks. While there she found a blind colored uncle, very old, who could do nothing but make rag rugs, and she rustled up from her school friends rags enough to keep him busy for a season. The last engagement she tried to make was to take the guests at the county home out for a car ride. And the last endeavor of her life was to try to get a rest room for colored girls in the High School. She found one girl reading in the toilet, because there was no better place for a colored girl to loaf, and it inflamed her sense of injustice and she became a nagging harpie to those who, she thought, could remedy the evil. The poor she had always with her, and was glad of it. She hungered and thirsted for righteousness; and was the most impious creature in the world. She joined the Congregational Church without consulting her parents; not particularly for her soul's good. She never had a thrill of piety in her life, and would have hooted at a

"testimony." But even as a little child she felt the church was an agency for helping people to more of life's abundance, and she wanted to help. She never wanted help for herself. Clothes meant little to her. It was a fight to get a new rig on her; but eventually a harder fight to get it off. She never wore a jewel and had no ring but her High School class ring, and never asked for anything but a wrist watch. She refused to have her hair up; though she was nearly 17. "Mother," she protested, "you don't know how much I get by with, in my braided pigtails that I could not, with my hair up." Above every other passion of her life was her passion not to grow up, to be a child. The tom-boy in her, which was big, seemed to loath to be put away forever in skirts. She was a Peter Pan, who refused to grow up.

Her funeral yesterday at the Congregational Church was as she would have wished it; no singing, no flowers save the big bunch of red roses from her Brother Bill's Harvard classmen—Heavens, how proud that would have made her! and the red roses from the Gazette force —in vases at her head and feet. A short prayer, Paul's beautiful essay on "Love" from the Thirteenth Chapter of First Corinthians, some remarks about her democratic spirit by her friend, John H. J. Rice, pastor and police judge, which she would have deprecated if she could, a prayer sent down for her by her friend, Carl Nau, and opening the service the slow, poignant movement from Bethoven's Moonlight Sonata, which she loved, and closing the service a cutting from the joyously melancholy first movement of Tschaikowski's Pathetic Symphony, which she liked to hear in certain moods on the phonograph; then the Lord's Prayer by her friends in the High School.

That was all.

For her pall-bearers only her friends were chosen; her Latin teacher — W. L. Holtz; her High School principal, Rice Brown; her doctor, Frank Foncannon; her friend, W. W. Finney; her pal at the Gazette office, Walter Hughes; and her brother Bill. It would have made her smile to know that her friend, Charley O'Brien, the traffic cop, had been transferred from Sixth and Commercial to the corner near the church to direct her friends who came to bid her good-bye.

A rift in the clouds in a gray day threw a shaft of sunlight upon her coffin as her nervous, energetic little body sank to its last sleep. But the soul of her, the glowing, gorgeous, fervent soul of her, surely was flaming in eager joy upon some other dawn.
—W. A. W.

Acknowledgements

Mary White's father told only part of her story. Many reminders of her remain in archives and in the hands of individuals. I am indebted to Mary's niece, Barbara White Walker, and Mrs. Walker's son, Christopher White Walker, for again allowing us to use archival materials and the words of their grandfather and great-grandfather. Thanks to Doug Weaver of Kansas City Star Books for supporting this project. Fortune smiled when the Dodds, Monroe and Jean, took on editing and designing another book on the Whites. Thank you to John Atherton for sharing the charming postcard and letter Mary sent her teacher, his aunt, so many years ago. Heather Wade, Emporia State University archivist, again served as a top-notch research companion on this book, and her reading room supervisor, Michelle Franklin, joined in the fun with her many "finds." Brenda Lavington of the Lyon County Historical Archives, Greg Jordan at the Lyon County Historical Museum, Marcia Fox at the Kansas State Historical Society and the staff at the University of Kansas Spencer Research Library all aided in the gathering of images and material for this book. Roger Heineken, Cheryl Unruh, Nick Gronseth, the William Allen White Community Partnership and other fine Emporia folks continued the cheerleading as this book progressed as did Roy Bird, my children's literature friends and fellow librarians. My husband, Paul, deserves much credit for his patient listening to read-alouds as well as for maintaining his steadfast support.

My friend Mary Downing Hahn told me Mary White was her girlhood hero. I wrote this book for the children who wanted to learn more about her, but there is a whole generation that remembers Mary White from their childhood. I hope this book introduces this remarkable girl to a new generation and completes her story for another.

SOURCE NOTES

Anecdotes about Mary used in this book came from these sources:

Broucek, Karen and Kristen Roberts. *We Remember Mary White*. Topeka West Oral History Project, 1978. Kansas State Historical Society. (Interviews with one of Mary's teacher's and twelve of her classmates and townspeople.)

Carle, Cecil. "The Legend of Mary White." Unpublished manuscript. Emporia State University Archives. (Cecil witnessed Mary's triumphant climb of Long's Peak.)

Morris, Loverne. "Life at Red Rocks, 1900-1918". *Kanhistique*. April, 1979. (Loverne observed Mary enjoying neighborhood life, including Mary and her horse entering Grandma White's front door.)

Pocher, H. Richard. Letter to William Allen White, undated. William Allen White Collection, University of Kansas Spencer Research Library. (Mr. Pocher writes to Mr. White on the occasion of his 70th birthday in 1938 and discloses a long-kept secret.)

Powers, Ann Randolph. "Reminiscences of William Allen White" (audio recording). Emporia State University Archives, Emporia, Kansas. (Ann witnessed Mary's earliest attempts at driving and became the "designated driver" of the Whites' first car.)

White, William Allen. *The Autobiography of William Allen White*. New York: Macmillan, 1946.

Letter to J.J. Duncan Jr., Estes Park, about Cricket can be found in *Selected Letters of William Allen White*, edited by Walter Johnson. New York: Henry Holt and Co., 1947, p. 216.